TOM WATSON'S

# GETTING BACK TO BASICS

# TOM WATSON'S
# GETTING BACK TO BASICS

### By Tom Watson
### with Nick Seitz

POCKET BOOKS

New York   London   Toronto   Sydney   Tokyo   Singapore

Published by:

Golf Digest/Tennis, Inc.
A New York Times Company,
5520 Park Avenue, Box 395
Trumbull, CT 06611-0395

and

POCKET BOOKS, a division of Simon & Schuster Inc.
1230 Avenue of the Americas
New York, NY 10020

Book Design by Nick DiDio

Photography by Dom Furore

Illustrations by Anthony Ravielli

ISBN: 0-671-74293-0

Library of Congress Cataloging-in-Publication Number: 91-76595

First Golf Digest/Tennis, Inc. and Pocket Books
hardcover printing January 1992

10  9  8  7  6  5  4  3  2  1

Printed in the U.S.A.

*I dedicate this book to all those from whom I learned the elements and techniques of the golf swing. I especially want to thank Byron, Stan and the Monday gangsomes who taught me how to compete—but most importantly taught me how to love this best of all games.*

# CONTENTS

# INTRODUCTION
# BY LEE TREVINO

It's funny how little things stick in a man's mind. One of my first memories of Tom Watson is from the 1974 Jackie Gleason Inverrary Classic, and it had nothing to do with the tournament. On Wednesday, the day of the pro-am, I was driving my car to the club when I happened to glance over at a course near Inverrary Country Club. All alone in a practice bunker was Tom Watson, a green kid who, I'd been told, hit the ball too wildly to last on the PGA Tour. I barely noticed; I went ahead and played my round in the pro-am. But when I left the course five hours later, I looked over at that golf course and damn if Watson wasn't in the same bunker, still practicing sand shots.

That told me something about Tom Watson. A kid with that kind of devotion to practice, that much determination to succeed, is going to find a way to make it. And he did. Seventeen years later, he stands behind only Jack Nicklaus in my mind as the best player I've ever seen.

All that time spent in practice bunkers, on putting greens and on driving ranges is what makes Tom so well qualified to write a book on how to play this devilish game. He's an incredible perfectionist. I don't believe there's an active player on the PGA Tour who knows golf better than Tom Watson. He has a deep understanding of the golf swing and has the intelligence and communication skills necessary to impart his knowledge to the average golfer.

Tom's approach to instruction is solid—he stresses the fundamentals. It shows in his swing. Tom's back is square to the target at the top of his backswing, his club parallel to the ground. He has great leg drive and keeps his hands quiet through impact. Tom is not a big man—he weighs about 165 pounds—but he is an extremely long hitter because there's no wasted motion in his swing.

Pay special attention to what Tom has to say about the grip. If you have a bad grip, sooner or later you'll pay for it. My grip isn't exactly classic, and I can't help but think that if I'd learned a good grip through a book like this one 35 years ago, I would have had an easier time of things with my career.

Tom's swing today is better than it's ever been, but he never stops questing. Not long ago I was sitting around late at night and the phone rang. It was Tom. "Lee, the ball's going right on me," he said. "What do you think? Is it the shaft? Too much weight in the clubhead? You see anything funny in my swing?"

We talked for an hour. That's what makes Tom special. He is naturally inquisitive and he's not afraid to ask questions. Like all great players, he's always thinking, always trying to figure out a way to get better. The winner in all this is you. What follows can't help but improve your game, and I'm proud of my friend Tom for writing it.

# PREFACE
# BY NICK SEITZ

"Kill the pig!" Tom Watson shouted at me. "Kill the pig!"

We were playing a fun round at the grand old Greenbrier resort, and a genteel group of tourists stopped its bird-watching in shocked wonderment. Kill the pig?

It is an expression Watson picked up from a pro-am partner who used it to remind himself to release the clubhead aggressively through the ball. Watson loves to think metaphorically about the golf swing, and whenever I see him he will ask if I am killing the pig.

It's a tribute to Watson that he enjoys playing with us average golfers and helping us. That makes him rare for a superstar who has won eight major championships. Says his publishing friend Tony Wimpfheimer, "Tom has the requisite great champion's ego, but he has a passion for the game on all levels."

The tattered folk saying holds that those who can, do, and those who can't, teach. Watson can do and can teach. I've watched him play an outing with six foursomes and improve everybody on the course a few minutes at a time. He cares about them, and he won't let up until he finds a way to get through to them, even if it means jolting a contingent of bird watchers.

If there is one main tenet Watson stresses repeatedly, both in person and in this book, it is his belief that you must vigorously rotate your left forearm during the swing to play strong golf. He gives us several thoughts, drills and images to accomplish his key move. I and hundreds of other weekend golfers who have been exposed to his instruction know it works when executed correctly.

Watson and I agreed this book should be simple, visual and different from past basics books. You should be able to take it to the practice range with you and use it. It's organized so you can learn the swing or refresh yourself on the swing in a logical, easy-to-track order. Anthony Ravielli's famous artwork drives home the major points of each chapter on a fundamental. At the end of each chapter, Watson picks a tour pro he rates the best at executing that chapter's fundamental and we see each member of this modern all-star swing team in action. Chapters on drills and images will help you master and remember the basics. The chapter on tempo pulls them together into a flowing whole, and concludes with extensive sequence photography of that old smoothie Sam Snead, Watson's tempo model. The book concludes with full sequences of Watson's own swing from five separate camera angles.

I have been collaborating with Watson for Golf Digest magazine for about 15 years. He talks into my tape recorder the substance of everything that appears under his byline. The material is then transcribed by Lois Hains. Watson will read the transcript, and we go back and forth refining his thoughts until both of

**Watson and collaborator enjoy a fun round.**

us are satisfied. He will suggest art ideas and approve artist Ravielli's preliminary sketches. Among the credits, I'd like to list the fellow who invented the fax machine. He's made this prolonged creative process infinitely simpler and faster. Now if we could just get an instruction manual Watson and I can comprehend...

I also should thank, in behalf of myself and Watson, Jack McDermott and Doug Hardy of the Golf Digest books department for their encouragement and deadline threats. Watson's manager, Chuck Rubin, helped us work within the demands of his client's dizzying schedule. Linda Hipski, my assistant, coordinated everything at my end with unflagging enthusiasm. Nick DiDio, the art director of Golf Digest, designed the book and suddenly is driving the ball 30 yards farther.

I hope you enjoy the book and I hope it helps you as much as working with Watson has helped me. And remember to kill that pig!

# FOREWORD
# BY TOM WATSON

Einstein had to learn to add and subtract before he developed the theory of relativity. A golfer has to learn to grip the club and set up to the ball before he can drive the ball far and straight. In science or golf, the basics are crucial. In golf, the basics *are* the golf swing.

This book consists of a series of basic swing keys, presented one at a time in the order you need to learn them. When you take a lesson, it's difficult to concentrate on more than one thing at a time. The beginner can follow this book step-by-step to build a solid swing. The advanced player can use it as an orderly reference guide and refresher course. As we get older and lose distance and touch, we need to rely even more on good swing basics.

Tour pros are always practicing the basics. Fans think we are out there on the range working on esoteric new theories. What we're out there working on is stimulating old stuff like placing the left hand on the club correctly and aiming the clubface squarely at the target.

To the pro, everything about the swing is a basic; everything is a fundamental. When you are playing poorly, golf gets too complicated. When you are playing well, it's very uncomplicated, because you are executing the fundamentals well and the fundamentals are uncomplicated. There is one way to stand up to the ball on a level lie. Period. When a pro's swing goes off, he goes right back to the basics.

The idea is to make every swing as simple as possible. Ultimately we want a swing that will repeat from one shot to another under pressure, whether we're playing for $200,000 first money on the tour or a $2 nassau.

I don't have any shortcuts to a sound, repeatable swing. If you're looking for quick fixes, you've come to the wrong book. Each fundamental must be learned fully, which takes time and practice. If you don't hold the club correctly and set up to the ball correctly, I can't teach you. I've heard Jack Nicklaus many times in clinics and exhibitions tell weekend golfers that if they execute the grip and setup correctly he can teach them. If they don't, he can't. If they don't, their swings will be full of compensatory moves for a bad grip and setup, and they won't be able to repeat those makeshift swings.

If your grip and setup give you a sound foundation, I think you can swing the club a lot of different ways and be consistent. Grip and setup are boring, static basics, but they affect everything that happens during your swing.

I devote a lot of space in this book to the grip because it is the hardest thing for a beginner to learn and the hardest thing for an advanced player to change. Please realize it's going to take time—quite a bit of time—to perfect the grip. I want you to do nothing but grip a club an hour a day for a week. Don't even swing the club—just get comfortable with the feel of the grip. Do it while you're watching television to take some of the tedium out of it. But do it.

When new golfers ask me how to get started in the game, I tell them to do two things. The first is to go buy a club. The second is to go get a lesson on the grip from a good teaching professional. Most people want a less rigorous answer. Right away they want to hit it as far as John Daly downwind. They don't want to hear that golf is not an easy game to learn and that you have to go to Swing High School before you can go to Swing University. You have to work and work and work with the grip until it feels comfortable.

I learned the grip from Harry Vardon, though he was dead before I was born. His grip has been passed down by teachers and books and golf magazines and is still the accepted standard. I want to emphasize that the grip chapter and the rest of this book are not Tom Watson pontificating about the golf swing. This book is what Tom Watson has learned about the golf swing from more people than he could think to credit.

I began learning from my father, a club champion, and then from Stan

Thirsk, a Kansas City club pro. When I was a teenager I was lucky enough to get to play with the club pros in the Kansas City area on Monday, their day off: pros like Duke Gibson and Herman Scharlau and Harold Reid. We'd get up a gangsome and go play. "Where are we playing next week?" they'd say afterward, and everybody would look forward to it. Those were exciting times for a kid, some of the best times of my life. I learned from those men, who learned from their forebears. What they taught me is laced through this book.

The most important advice they gave me when I left to join the tour was to study the better players and try to play practice rounds with them. I took it to heart. I remember playing in a satellite tournament near the Heritage Classic on Hilton Head Island, and after my round one day I went over and followed Jack Nicklaus for 18 holes at the big tournament. I was impressed right away by his fundamentally sound grip and his wonderful swing tempo. Later I was able to play a lot with Jack, observe him up close and ask him questions. The answers helped me improve. At any level of the game, it's smart to play with better players and learn from them.

After I became a more accomplished player, Byron Nelson helped me greatly. I still go back to Byron and to things he's taught me. He's as wonderful a person as he is a teacher.

To a very real extent, then, I've learned everything I know about the swing from other people. What I've done with my swing—and what I've done with this book—is put together various pieces of information in the simplest, most useful package I could. The parts of a swing have to blend into a cohesive whole. You have to understand the assembly process so that in the end you can become your own best teacher and fix your swing when it breaks down.

Your swing has to become second nature so that in competition you can focus on the shot you need to play and the target. Ray Floyd was asked what he would think about if he had a three-foot putt to win the U.S. Open. He said he wouldn't think about anything—he'd just let his instincts take over. That's where I want you to be when you finish this book.

As the book took shape, I wanted to come up with hopefully memorable images of the swing that would make it seem less an array of parts and more an overall movement. One of them, dealing with the rotation of the left forearm, I have positioned first in the book, even before the Grip chapter. I think it's that important. It will recur as you go through the book. It isn't a common concept, although I suspect it's at the heart of Ben Hogan's swing theory and may even be his long-debated "secret."

I hope you take this image and the other instruction that follows and practice it diligently to make your swing the best it can be. You will enjoy this captivating game to the fullest. And on a few lustrous days you will hit solid shot after solid shot and probably feel as if you've discovered the theory of relativity.

# THE
# SWING
# STEP
# BY
# STEP

I believe the rotation of the left forearm mainly controls the golf swing (if you're right-handed). It's my primary image of the swing as an overall motion. I'd like you to keep it in mind as we march through the fundamentals from grip to follow-through.

You can feel the correct rotation of the left forearm by resting the edge of your left hand on a tabletop. That's your address position. Now, as this artwork demonstrates, rotate your left forearm clockwise until your palm is flat on the table. That's the extent of your forearm rotation on the backswing. Next, rotate the forearm back to its original position. That's impact. Finally, rotate the forearm so the back of your hand is flat on the table. You've released the club.

Your left wrist should hinge or "break" up and down a bit during the swing, but it does not bend sideways and break down. It stays firm.

If you rotate your left forearm correctly, you can hit the ball hard with your right hand. You won't slice the ball.

There's a lot more to the swing than just rotating the left forearm—but rotating the left forearm is my No. 1 key.

Through-swing

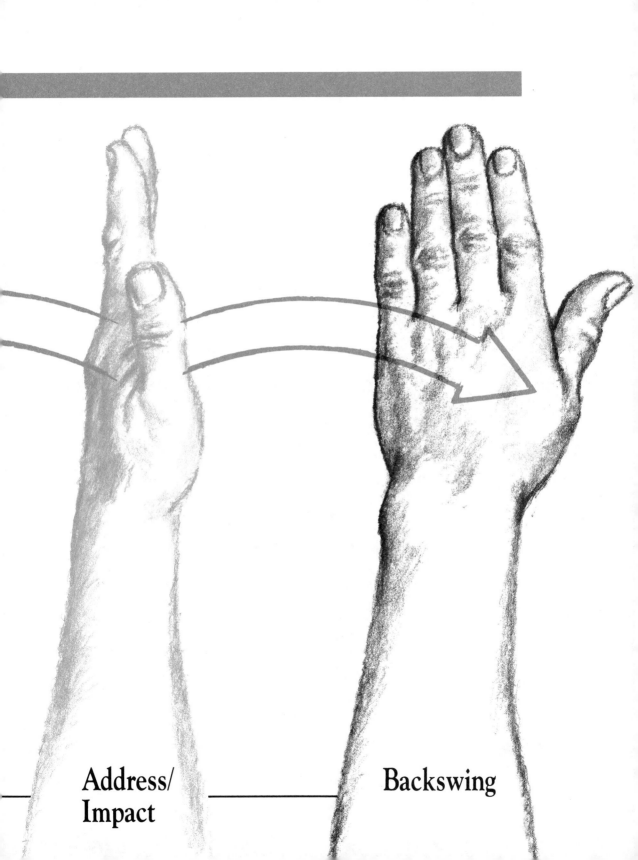

Address/
Impact

Backswing

# THE GRIP

The grip is not the most exciting subject in golf instruction—but it is the most important. Your hands connect you to the club. A good swing begins with a good grip, and a bad swing begins with a bad grip. I would say that 95 percent of the leisure golfers I see lack a fundamentally sound grip. As a result, they will never be able to play nearly to their potential.

For all my full shots and most of my short shots I use the Vardon overlapping grip, which is named after the great Harry Vardon, who won the British Open six times. The little finger of my right hand overlaps my left hand in the indentation between the left index finger and middle finger. The seven fingers I have on the club form a cohesive unit.

I like the Vardon grip because it unifies the hands and helps them work together. I'm not saying it's the only way to hold the club. The interlocking grip (the little finger of the right hand interweaves with the forefinger of the left

**1. The club rests diagonally across the palm of my left hand.**

**2. The left thumb runs down the right center of the shaft (not on top).**

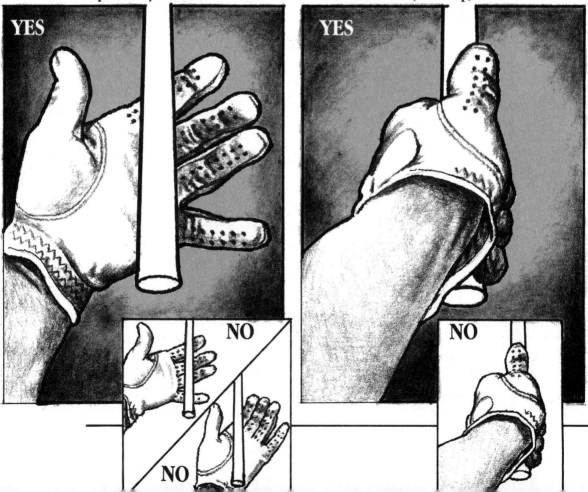

hand) is favored by no less than Jack Nicklaus, who has small hands. He believes it's a more natural, solid grip. The 10-finger or baseball grip also has merit. Its supporters think it promotes more wrist action, for one thing.

In the Vardon grip, the club runs diagonally across the inside of my left hand, from about the first joint of the forefinger down to just under the pad of the hand. My left thumb goes down the right center of the shaft—not straight down the top of the club. If you put your thumb straight down the shaft, you will find it too difficult to hinge the club upward on the backswing and to release it through the ball on the downswing. Set your left thumb off-center to the right.

There is a debate among golf technocrats over whether we should grip the club with a "long left thumb" or a "short left thumb." I prefer a short thumb. I don't think you should extend your left thumb down the handle, because then you have a problem gripping correctly with your right hand. The right hand will

**3. In the right hand the club lays in the fingers, not the palm.**

**4. Here is how my assembled grip looks to me.**

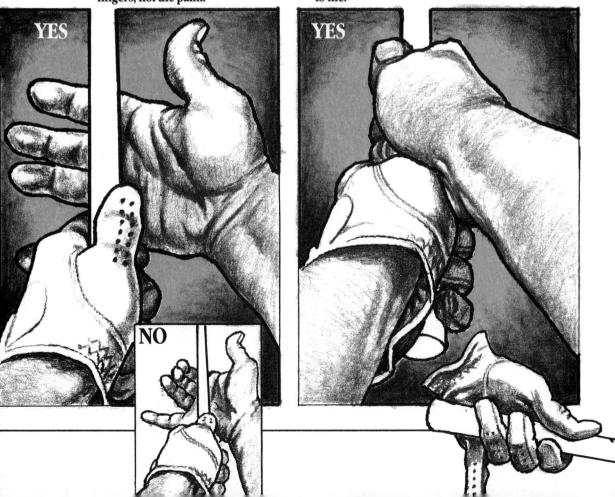

tend to go too far under the club.

You don't want the club too much in the palm of the left hand or too much in the fingers, or else the club can slip and cause your left hand to break down during the swing. The left hand and arm need to be the firm fulcrum that establishes the radius of your swing. Left-hand dominance is an overall key to the swing, and it is initiated in the grip.

The club lies in the fingers of the right hand, not the palm. It runs across the ring and middle fingers and cleanly against the index finger. You will see a narrow gap between the middle finger and index finger. That gap lets the right forefinger and thumb, which rests down the left center of the shaft, "cradle" the club for greater control and feel. The right little finger overlaps the left hand. A second overlap in the Vardon grip is the lifeline of my right hand overlapping the thumb of my left hand.

When you put your hands together on the club, notice the two "V"s formed by your thumbs and forefingers. In an ideal grip, the left "V" should point approximately toward your right eye, and the right "V" approximately toward your chin. You will see two knuckles showing on the back of your left hand. This is a neutral grip, neither too weak (the hands turned more to your left) nor too strong (hands turned more to your right).

It is a good player's grip. A weaker player might try turning his hands more clockwise on the grip, so that three knuckles show on the left hand. This "stronger" grip will encourage the hands to be more active in the hitting zone, helping the clubface return to square and diminishing the chances of a slice.

Over all, I would like to see you grip the club mainly in your fingers, as opposed to your palms. First of all, your fingers transmit more feel. If you reach into your pocket and pull out a coin, you feel it with your fingers. You don't feel with your palms. Second, you don't have to grip as hard with your fingers as you would with your palms, so you are much more flexible in your swing. You can whip the club through the ball with your hands and generate more clubhead speed, which means more distance.

Have you ever watched the way a good baseball hitter grips the bat? He "milks" the handle with his fingers, moving them up and down, up and down, so he doesn't get stiff. He's relaxed and ready to swing the bat freely.

## GRIP PRESSURE

Generally speaking you need enough grip pressure to control the club throughout the swing but not so much that you create tension, especially in your forearms. You must hold the club firmly, but you don't have to squeeze it hard. I try to be firm with my hands but relaxed in my forearms. The forearms have to be very light and active in the swing. If they tighten up, the shoulders also tighten up, and you won't be able to turn fully enough.

If your grip pressure is good, you will be able to swing rhythmically. A collection of mechanical movements will blend together and your swing will flow. You will feel oily, as Sam Snead likes to say, and you will hit the ball both straighter and farther. You will know where the clubhead is during the swing, and that's crucial.

What is the correct grip pressure for you?

Just enough to control the club. When you are practicing, loosen your grip pressure—back off until the club is almost falling out of your hands. Then firm it up a little bit and you should have your best grip pressure. I am willing to wager it's not as tight as it was before. Start with the lightest possible grip pressure and gradually increase it until you find the amount of pressure that lets you control the club without it slipping at all in your hands. The club must never slip in your hands. If you develop blisters, the club is slipping.

There are specific pressure points to appreciate as you learn to grip and swing the club. Essentially the left hand is on the club to guide it and the right hand supplies touch and power. The left hand thus holds the club more firmly than the right.

I apply most of the gripping pressure with the last three fingers of my left hand, particularly the little finger. The little finger is the most vital pressure point for a good, firm grip. Try taking it off the club and you'll quickly realize that you are barely able to support the club. If I can keep the last three fingers of my left hand solidly on the club, I won't lose it during the swing. I apply as much pressure in those three fingers as I can, short of causing my left arm to tighten. My left forearm is firm but not tense. The left thumb and forefinger exert almost no pressure at all.

Let's talk about right-hand pressure. I apply very little pressure with my right hand, just enough to keep it from slipping. The ring and middle fingers are the anchors that hold the right hand in place against the left and unify the activity of the two hands during the swing. There is virtually no pressure coming from the right thumb and forefinger. You may have noticed that Jack Nicklaus actually lets his right forefinger come off the club at the top of his swing. Ben Hogan practiced leaving his right thumb and forefinger off the club.

If you grip tightly with your right thumb and forefinger, you tend to tense your entire right side and sabotage your swing. I learned that reality back in 1977, when I made a point of lightening the grip pressure in my right hand. I had my first big year, winning five tournaments including the Masters and the British Open.

It's good to strive for an even grip pressure from address to follow-through. It won't happen, because your grip pressure will intensify during the swing, but it's a sensible goal. If you start with a grip that is too tight, it will only get worse as you swing. Lighter is better than tighter when it comes to grip pressure.

## GRIPPING AND SHOTMAKING

It is easier to hit the ball from left to right with a weak grip and easier to hook the ball with a strong grip. The key is to adjust the position of your hands on the club *without changing the position of the clubface*! It's too easy in gripping the club to rotate your hands clockwise to hook the ball and at the same time rotate the clubface into an open position. Your chances of getting the clubface back to square at impact are slim, and your chances of getting it closed so you can hit a hook are even slimmer. Whenever you alter your grip to maneuver the ball, make sure you keep the clubface aiming squarely.

You also can influence the flight of the ball through grip pressure. If I want to make sure I don't curve the ball too much from right to left, I will grip more firmly with my left hand and less firmly with my right hand. But if I want to be sure I can hit the ball from right to left, I will lighten my grip pressure in my left hand so my right hand takes over at the bottom of the swing and makes the ball hook. Since most of you slice the ball, you might want to experiment in practice with that second technique. But you still need to grip firmly enough with the left hand to control the club.

The size of the grips on your clubs—the thickness of the material—also can affect the shape of your shots. The thicker the grip, the harder it is to rotate your hands through the ball and hook it, but the easier it is to fade the ball. The thinner the grip, the easier it is to rotate your hands and hook, but the harder it is to slice. If you are in that great majority of golfers who slice, you might want to consider thinner grips. Putting on new grips is not difficult, and I do it myself in my basement workshop. You should regrip your clubs—or have them re-gripped—at least once a year so they don't get too smooth and slippery.

## MAKING A GRIP CHANGE

If you decide to improve the position of your hands on the club, be aware that you will be making perhaps the most difficult adjustment there is in the game. You have been setting your hands on the club in a certain way that feels comfortable to you even if it's incorrect. When you grip the club correctly, it isn't going to feel as comfortable for some time.

Grip and regrip a club as often as you can at home to get accustomed to the new feeling. Keep a club by your chair and grip it as you watch golf on television. Do this during the off-season and your new grip should be feeling natural by spring.

Do exercises to strengthen your hands, too—squeeze a rubber ball, for example. Working on your grip is a wise investment in your game's future. Remember, good golf begins with a good grip.

Best grip:
Ben Crenshaw

I almost always can predict when my 15-handicap friends are going to hit a good shot, because they will be set up well. Their posture will be good. Your posture virtually dictates how you will strike the ball.

Posture is a problem for most players, but it is probably the simplest problem to correct. Since posture directly affects your balance and the plane of your swing, it is extremely important. I advocate an elementary 1-2-3 approach to establishing good posture.

**1.** Stand up straight, with your feet slightly wider than your shoulders. Open—toe out—your right foot about 15 degrees and your left foot about 30 degrees. This is so you can turn more away from the ball and back through it.

**2.** Bend from the waist. Now you have created a sound spine angle and can swing down at the ball. You will want to maintain this spine angle throughout the swing. It stabilizes you and keeps your head from bobbing up and down. There's no slumping in the lower back at all. If you feel at this stage as though there is too much weight on your toes, it's only because there is. We'll soon rectify that.

**3.** Flex your knees and stick out your rear end. This final stage balances you and puts ballast in your swing. You should almost feel as though you're sitting down. If you fall forward as you swing, you know that your butt isn't sticking out enough. Stick it out until you feel a little tension in the small of your back.

Your weight will still be toward your toes, but not too much. You're poised to move. Your lower body can work easier. You'll be able to stay down on the ball making contact. No good athlete gets his weight back on his heels. A fast runner is on the balls of his feet. A basketball player is. A football player is.

I'd rather see you put too much weight toward your toes than err toward your heels. If you're back on your heels starting your swing, there's no way you can turn your hips correctly. You'll have to just lift the club with your arms and make a weak swing. You'll straighten up and fall back. If you fall forward, at least you can swing your arms down the line with some speed. You should be able to tap your heels on the ground easily if your weight is toward your toes.

Here's how you can check your knee flex. Your knees should be flexed enough that they are just about over your toes as you look down. Your legs will be flexible from that position. A warning: Even though your knees are flexed, you can still put too much weight on your heels. Be balanced on the balls of your feet, ready to go!

There's another positive result of flexing the knees and setting your weight on the balls of your feet. An active lower body keeps the head quiet. As my long-time friend and mentor Byron Nelson, who had the greatest year in golf history in 1945, has always put it, "Freedom down below keeps the head still." If your legs are stiff—if you have "cement legs" as I call them—and your weight is back

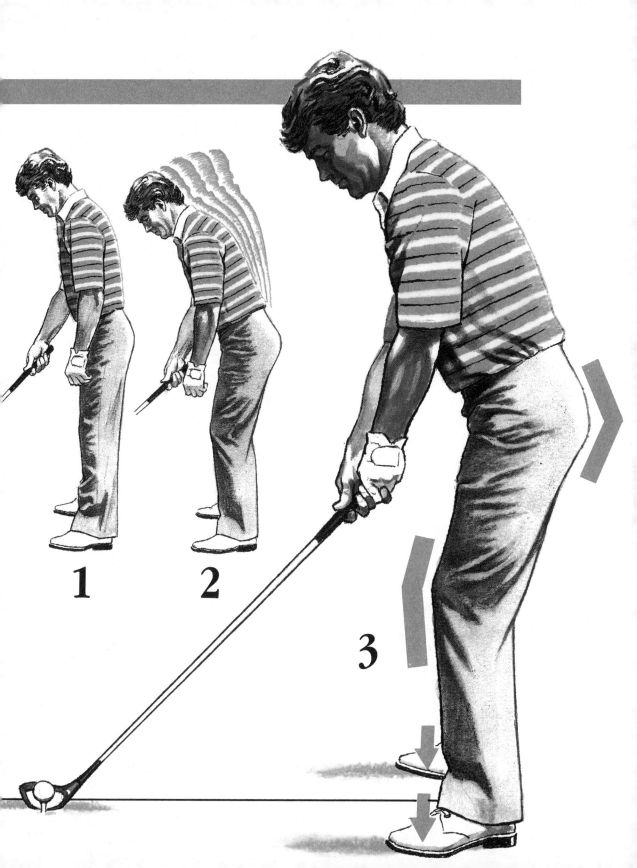

Best posture:
Nick Faldo

toward your heels, your head is going to move way too much.

Your weight should be distributed about equally between your feet. I like the way Jack Nicklaus exemplifies that and also how he positions his weight toward the insides of his feet. Jack's in wonderful balance.

Okay. You're bent from the waist, your knees are flexed so their edges are over your toes, your backside is stuck out, your weight is on the balls of your feet. Your body has taken on an accordion look. Your shins angle out, your thighs angle back in and your upper body angles out. The accordion is ready to play. From this posture you can let your arms hang naturally and comfortably, and that's where you'll grip the club. Your wrists will be semi-cocked already. If your left arm and the club form a straight line, your wrists are too high and you will swing stiff-armed.

You should never feel you have to reach for the ball, even with a driver, and you should never feel cramped either. Your arms should be able to swing in front of you in a relaxed manner, and from the setup posture we've talked about they will. Check your posture by turning sideways to a mirror. Be sure those arms are hanging naturally.

## COMMON SETUP FAULTS

The most frequent setup mistake I see is standing too erect. It happens typically with people who are short or who have weak legs or both.

If you are too erect, your arms hang too close to your body and you cannot swing them freely in front of you. Your arms might hit your legs. The club will go around behind you too soon and you won't be able to make a full, easy turn and coil on the backswing. Your swing is dominated by the arms having to work too hard without much help. You probably will spin out.

You must have enough bend at the waist to make an easy shoulder turn. The shoulders have to stay on plane. That means you cannot stand too erect.

At the other extreme, crouching and bending over too much result in a swing that's too upright. About all you can do is stick your arms straight up in the air. The club wants to move too vertically instead of around the body.

Bending excessively from the waist also is hard on the back, and this game isn't easy on the back anyway. Fuzzy Zoeller hurt his back in a basketball accident when he was young, but to swing a golf club from a deep crouch the way he does has to put extra stress on his back.

I would rather see somebody not bent over enough rather than bent over too much. Being too erect is a bad position, but at least you can go down from there and get to the ball. When you are bent over too much, you are apt to lift up coming into the ball and make poor contact.

# AIM AND ALIGNMENT

How you line up a golf shot pretty much determines where it will go. Aim and alignment are factors you can control before you swing and they deserve extra care. You aim the clubface and align your body, in that order.

Aiming the clubface is like aiming a gun. If you don't aim the face accurately, you won't hit your target. I recommend the Jack Nicklaus method of spot-aiming. I don't use it completely myself, but I'm convinced it's the best way. It's like spot-bowling. Instead of concentrating on a distant target (the pins), a bowler focuses on a close-in target (a spot on the lane).

Jack is painstaking with his preshot aiming procedure, and he goes through it the same way every time. He's practiced it by the hour. He prepares to hit every range ball as though it were a shot to decide the U.S. Open.

You should start from a few yards behind the ball and pick out your intended target line. You are looking out over the ball to your target. You get a much clearer picture of the line from behind the ball than from the side, where you will address it. You'd aim a gun sighting down the barrel, right?

We'll assume you want to hit the ball straight rather than deliberately curve it—in any case you are selecting the line on which you plan to start the shot. (If you were going to fade the ball, the line would point left of your target, while if you were going to draw the ball, it would point right.)

You have identified your target line and are still standing behind the ball. Now you want to identify an intermediate target or aiming spot just a few feet in front of the ball. It might be a light blade of grass or a leaf or a small stick. You build your aim and alignment off this spot.

Keep referring to your spot as you move into your stance from behind the ball. Aim the clubface first, then align your body. Too many people align the body first, which causes faulty aiming. Be sure you don't walk past the ball in aiming the face. You circle into the ball from behind, checking your intermediate spot as you do. Aim the clubface squarely at your spot. Aim the bottom line of the clubface to be sure it's square.

Your right foot is roughly in position. Spread your left foot out into place, and adjust your right foot so you're comfortable. Be sure as you take your stance that you do not change the attitude of the clubface. It must remain square to the spot in front of the ball. Grip the club gently to keep it perpendicular to the spot.

Look up and check to see that your clubface, your spot and your ultimate target off in the distance are all in line. If you fear they are not, back off and start your aiming and aligning process all over again. Go behind the ball and take it step-by-step. I don't want to encourage slow play, because there's far too much of that already, but you have to get this part of the game right or you cannot play acceptable golf. Be brisk, but be exacting.

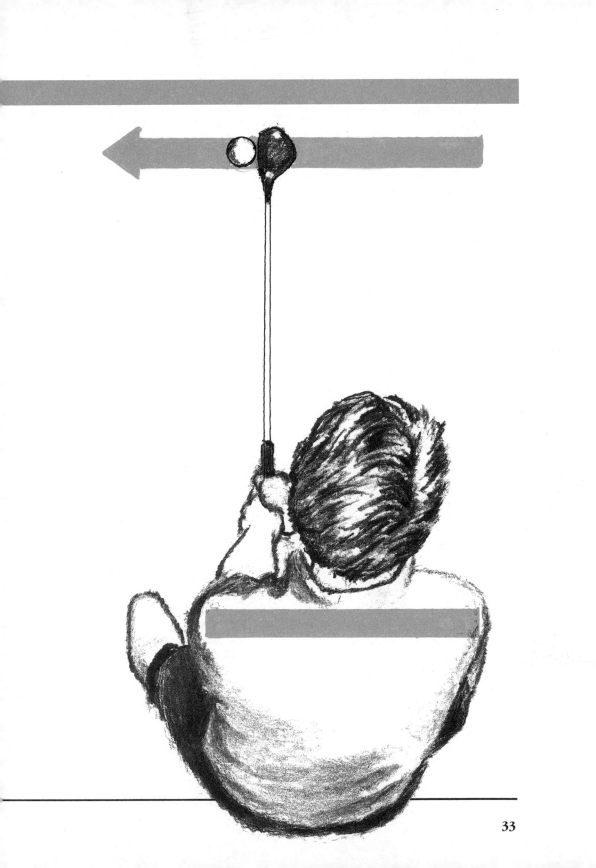

**Best aiming procedure:
Jack Nicklaus**

## THE BODY IS PARALLEL LEFT

Basically your body should be aligned parallel to your target line at address. Imagine a pair of railroad tracks. The ball and your target line are on the outside track. Your feet are lined up on the inside track. Your feet, knees, hips and shoulders are aligned parallel or square to the target line.

Have you heard the golf teaching expression "parallel left"? Well, it means exactly what we are talking about. Your clubface is aimed at the target and your body is aligned parallel left of the target. A common fault is aligning the body at the target. Think about it a moment. If your body is aligned at the target, then your clubface almost certainly is aiming to the right of the target! Your body should be aligned somewhat left of the target, so the clubface can aim straight at it. Then you can make a natural swing without having to compensate and try to pull your shot back in the proper direction.

A good way to monitor your alignment is by placing two clubs on the ground when you practice. You see the top pros do it all the time, but for some reason 18-handicappers don't seem to want to be bothered. Put one club straight out from the ball toward the target. Put the other club along your toe line. The clubs should be parallel. You can rest the club you are going to swing across the tops of your thighs and then across your chest to see that your entire body is square. Memorize the feeling of a square alignment.

Your eye position also is important. It's possible to align your body accurately, but cause yourself problems when you look at your target before you start your swing, especially if you lift your head. Your eyes must be parallel like your body. If your eyes are cocked to the right of the target, that's most likely where your swing and the ball will go. If your eyes are cocked left, your swing and shot are prone to go left.

Even good tour players have trouble with their eye alignment. Lanny Wadkins tends to look to the right and hit push shots. Larry Mize has the opposite difficulty. I suspect it has something to do with a player's dominant eye, and it might make sense to get your eye doctor's thinking. But the point is to align your eyes the same as your feet, knees, hips and shoulders. It's helpful to swivel your head when you look at the target instead of lifting it. If you lift your head, you probably will lose your eye line. I've changed people's eye lines a couple of inches and seen them get amazingly improved results. Check your eye line by putting a club across it, lowering the club and relating it to your body lines.

Your overall head position is worth mentioning, too. Some amateurs sink their chins down into their chests as they line up a shot. They are defeated before they ever start to swing, because it's impossible for them to make a good turn. You want to swing your left shoulder under your chin on the backswing, and that's impossible if your chin gets in the way. Your head must be fairly erect at address and stay up during your swing. "Heads up!"

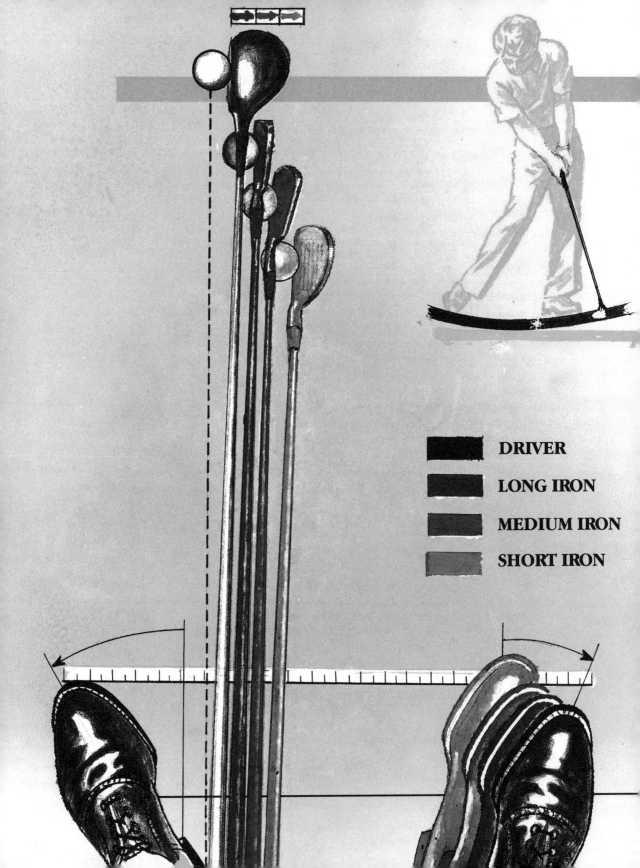

**DRIVER**

**LONG IRON**

**MEDIUM IRON**

**SHORT IRON**

# BALL POSITION

I advocate varying your ball position. The hitting zone is from the middle of the stance forward, and that's where you should put the ball. The longer the club, the farther forward you play the ball.

For a normal shot with a driver I want the ball opposite my left heel. For a wedge it will be back almost in the center of my stance. I measured some of my ball positions and found that the ball was an inch back of the heel for a 3-iron, another inch back for a 6-iron, and at least another inch back for a wedge.

Some days I am like Fuzzy Zoeller—I feel better with the ball all the way back of center with a wedge. But most of the time I'm comfortable with it just ahead of center. You move the ball back in your stance for a shorter club because you make a more descending swing. You cannot hit down on the ball effectively if it is off your left heel.

I know there are some great golf minds that advocate one standard ball position, just inside or opposite the left heel—Jack Nicklaus and Ben Hogan for two. But you have to be very athletic in your lower body to go down and get the ball. If it's in a bad lie, all the more reason to put the ball back in your stance. If you have trouble driving your legs and shifting your weight through the shot, you almost surely shouldn't play everything off your left heel. Most older players fall into this category. I've heard that Hogan moved the ball back as he got older, and I wouldn't be surprised to see Jack do it one day.

I like Hale Irwin's ball position. It's in mid-stance with a 5-iron, and he moves it up or back from there.

My left foot is essentially constant for every swing, driver through wedge. I change the width of my stance, and open or close my stance, by adjusting my right foot.

Best ball position:
Hale Irwin

My stance narrows and also opens as the club I am using gets shorter. It's 22 inches from the toe of my one foot to the toe of the other foot for a driver, 18 inches from toe to toe for a wedge. With the driver, my right foot is about an inch back of my stance line and 20 degrees toed out to the right. With the wedge, my right foot is about an inch in front of my stance line and a bit less toed out. I never want my right foot perpendicular to the line. It's too hard to turn my body on the backswing.

The essential reason for changing the right foot is to promote or restrict hip turn. A shorter club requires a more vertical swing, with less body pivot and more arm swing.

You use different swings in this game. Your rhythm should stay the same, but your arc changes. Golf is difficult for a tall man because he has to swing so vertically, and the body doesn't want to. It's easier for someone my size (5-9, 160 pounds) to swing every club freely.

To make good contact, though, my ball position must be fairly precise. I like to check it by putting a yardstick on the ground. Or I do it in the basement when I'm home during the off-season. Golf is a game of inches, none more important than these few that affect ball position.

How far should you stand from the ball? I get this question a lot. Remember when we talked about posture—getting you in balance with your weight toward your toes, your knees over your toes and your butt stuck out? You were going to grip the club where your arms hung and came together freely, in a comfortable position. From here the length of the club dictates how far you are away from the ball. You'll be farther from the ball with a driver than a 5-iron, but if you set up soundly that takes care of itself. Don't reach for the ball or feel cramped.

## NEXT: STARTING THE SWING

We've completed the preswing basics and we're ready to start the club swinging. Please remember that you cannot swing the club well if you don't grip it well and set up to the ball well. These "static" fundamentals are absolutely essential if you want to make good contact, and they are worth your complete and ongoing dedication. Practice them until they are second nature, and check them regularly with the means I've given you. If the best players in the world spend most of their considerable driving-range time working on preswing basics, it should tell you something.

## THE WAGGLE

Let's put the swing in motion, with the waggle and the takeaway.

The waggle is a sneak preview of your takeaway. It's a preliminary movement of the club back and forth from the ball to keep your wrists and forearms relaxed and to set the clubhead on the proper path. Waggle the club as many times as you feel necessary—I waggle twice myself. *Always* twice, as part of my preshot routine.

The waggle is usually more wristy than the takeaway, although Arnold Palmer and some other good players use the arms, too. They try to preview the takeaway precisely. That makes more sense than using only your wrists, if your wrists and forearms stay loose. If they stiffen, you won't be able to take the club back on the same route consistently enough.

When it comes to waggling, do as I say, not as I do. I waggle by picking the club up over the ball before I take it back, which accomplishes nothing. It's just a habit, and I'd prefer to waggle low and along the line of my takeaway. The club should flow along the ground in the direction you want it to go when you swing for real.

Normally the club path is straight back from the ball for a foot or so and then inside your target line. If you're advanced enough to curve your shots intentionally, adjust your waggle to maneuver the ball. For a hook, you want to swing the club back inside your normal path, so waggle to the inside. For a slice, you swing the club

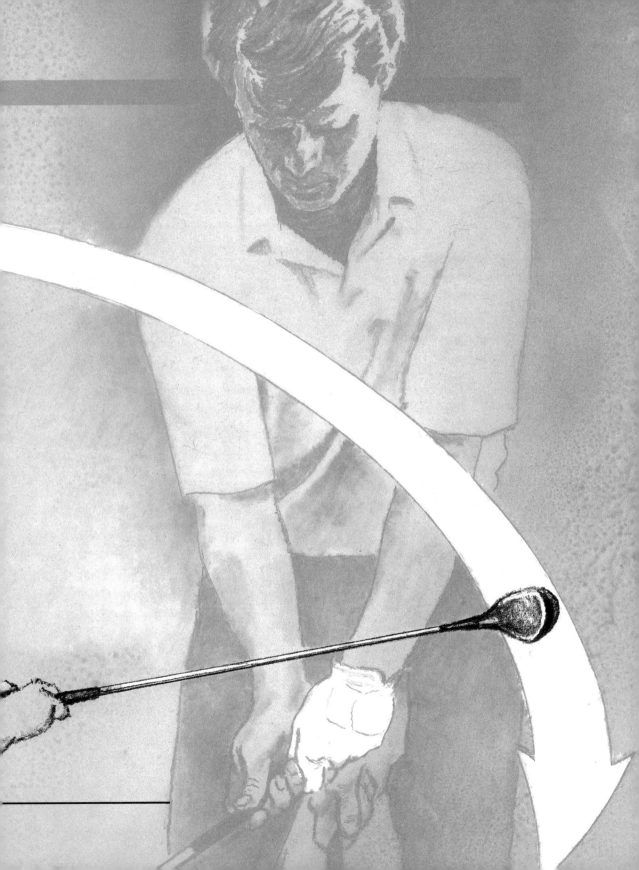

more outside, so waggle outside. That's a little more sophisticated.

A thoughtful, consistent waggle is more important to the golf swing than most players realize. Again, think of it as a sneak preview of your takeaway.

Actually, the waggle should blend smoothly into your takeaway. The waggle and takeaway are two parts of a flowing process as we try to avoid starting the swing from a standing start.

Stay in motion and don't come to a dead stop before taking the club back. *You need to make a fluid transition from your waggle into your backswing*, with what some people call a forward press.

I forward press just before I start my takeaway by kicking my right knee in slightly toward the target and then back. I also like the way Sam Snead, Jack Nicklaus and John Mahaffey swivel their heads around to the right, encouraging a free shoulder turn.

Many fine players shift the right knee slightly toward the target for a forward press. Gary Player has always done that quite conspicuously. It's his starter for the swing—the same as a car has a starter.

Gary says he feels he's previewing the correct impact position when he forward presses, because his weight shifts slightly onto his left foot, which is where he wants it at impact. But mainly he wants to keep moving from the time he takes a club out of the bag until the ball's on its way.

Whatever mannerism you develop, stay in motion—like a tennis player preparing to return serve. The reward is smoother swing rhythm.

**Best waggle:
Arnold Palmer**

When I start my backswing I want a feeling of "togetherness." My key is to *take the club away with the left arm, left hip and left knee working together.*

The swing starts in one piece. Arnold Palmer and Byron Nelson are great examples of the one-piece takeaway. Lanny Wadkins is quick on the draw, but he moves his left side back together. The left arm, hip and knee should turn together until the weight of the club causes the wrists to begin breaking. I like the hands and wrists to feel passive until they are about waist high. Then the wrists begin to hinge. The arms stay close to the body.

If your upper body starts the swing by itself, your lower body has to play catch-up, or vice versa. Your timing will be inconsistent. Synchronize the movement of the left arm, hip and knee as if you were trying to move a heavy rock on the end of a string.

I have the feeling—and it's literally a physical sensation—that the timing of my swing starts from the feet. The swing is initiated from the ground up. I feel with my feet. They tell me if I'm swinging in sync.

I like my feet to feel light and active, ready to move. If you don't use your feet early in the swing the club won't go back on an arc. You'll pick it up too abruptly with your hands.

Watch good golfers as they move into the swing. They lightly tap their heels up and down against the ground. Lifting the heels slightly this way helps establish a rhythm for the swing and keeps the lower body relaxed. It also keeps the weight from drifting too far toward the heels.

As the club is moved away from the ball, the weight begins to shift from the inside of the left foot to the inside of the right foot. The left foot begins to roll away from the target, pushing the left knee toward the right knee. The left ankle is bending inward as the arms move the club back from the ball. The feet and arms should be moving to the same rhythm.

It's a lot like dancing. Julius Boros, who won the United States Open twice and later won the PGA Championship at the amazing age of 48, was a splendid dancer and a wonderfully rhythmic swinger of a golf club. He eased into his swing as if he were dancing a relaxed waltz. He flowed into it. Julius always said he never let himself come to a stop. He stayed in motion.

The first 12 inches of your swing are the most important. That first foot establishes your tempo and your swing path. Take the club away smoothly and straight, and you are on your way to a good result. After a foot or so the club comes inside the target line and up.

It's possible to take the club away from the ball too slowly, but almost no one does. Most of us need to slow down on the takeaway.

After the first foot you have very little control over your swing—the rest is pretty much just reaction. But you can control the takeaway, and that's why it is so important that you execute it well and execute it the same way every time.

45

The purposes of the backswing are to store power and to put the club in position for the downswing. I want to make a complete turn on every full swing, getting my back to the target and my shoulders behind the ball.

If you are supple enough, *your shoulders should be turned 90 degrees at the top of the swing and your hips turned 45 degrees.* Coil your upper body until you feel like a taut spring ready to unwind.

Your weight shifts to your right side, but should never stray to the outside of your right foot—retaining the flex in your right knee throughout the backswing helps your center of gravity remain relatively stable.

I try to stay relaxed and smooth enough that my left hand and arm can control the club all the way to the top. Remember the important rotation of the left forearm we talked about early in the book, when you put your left hand on a table and went through the rotating motions to get a feel for it? I like that forearm rotation to be complete halfway through the backswing, by the time your arms reach horizontal. Your left palm would be flat on the table. From there you simply lift the club to the top with your left arm.

Keeping my left arm reasonably straight, I swing back until I can feel tension across the large muscles in my upper back, my left shoulder and my upper left arm. You also should feel tension at the top of the swing on the inside of your right leg, in the calf and especially in the thigh. If you don't have this feeling, you have let your weight get too far to the outside of your foot.

I do not consciously manipulate or lift the club with my hands. The feeling is that my shoulders are carrying the club back.

Most people are afraid to turn their shoulders far enough. "Where am I?" they worry. They aren't planted well enough on the right side. My center of gravity shifts a little to my right, but that isn't bad. The thing you don't want to do is shift your center of gravity to your left. My left heel's come up off the ground a little, which facilitates a good turn. It replants when I start back down. Letting the left heel come up makes it much easier to turn the shoulders behind the ball. The shoulders must finish the backswing every time.

If your shoulders complete their turn, your arms will complete their backswing. My shoulders are not over the ball at the top; they are behind the ball. Try to turn your left shoulder to where your right shoulder was at address.

At the top I like the left arm to be slotted between my head and my right shoulder—not too high nor too low. That way I won't have to make compensations on my downswing. That's the power position.

I try to swing back with my right side feeling soft. Now I can turn my right hip out of the way. That allows that left heel to come up on the backswing and promotes a bigger turn. My right side never gets in my way as I turn back—it folds passively under the left side.

There can be a danger in overturning the hips, but I almost never see

90°

45°

Shoulders

Hips

Best backswing:
Greg Norman

weekend golfers succumb to it. Turn that right hip and free up your swing!

How far back should you swing the club?

I sometimes get it below parallel to the ground, but I'd prefer it to be dead *parallel* to the ground or just short of it. At least I have some room to play with when old age catches up with me and shortens my swing. It would be worse to cut off the backswing prematurely and rush down. As long as the left side is in control, you can get away with dipping below parallel. Don January does and Ben Hogan did in the early part of his career.

My role model for turning smoothly and fearlessly has always been Sam Snead. He's almost 80 and he still turns better than most golfers half his age. His left heel comes up on the backswing and he makes an unrestricted hip turn.

Sam has a pet expression. He tells people "Turn and burn! Turn and burn!" He always did himself.

Sam says he tries to turn his shoulders and hips as a team. It helps his tempo and keeps his turn from getting too short, especially as he gets older. He contends that a big turn kept his career going so long, and can help you play better longer.

Sam, who's a fine teacher, tells slicers to force themselves to turn more: They don't turn enough on the backswing, he says, and then they overwork something coming down.

He stresses that you have to turn just as much on a tight driving hole as you do any other time. If you try to steer the ball, you probably won't hit it far enough or straight enough.

The instructor I've been working with recently, David Leadbetter, emphasizes the same themes I've heard from Sam. He wants the body fully turned and "loaded up" on the backswing. He thinks the hips should make a slight lateral shift as they turn. This prevents the hated reverse weight shift that ruins so many swings—the weight going toward the target on the backswing and then away from it on the downswing. David doesn't want an unwelcome sway; just a barely noticeable lateral shift. The angle of your spine stays constant.

# STARTING DOWN

If the backswing was pretty much programmed, the downswing is more reflexive. It consists of a series of effects rather than causes.

*My main thought is to start down with the hips.* I think about sliding and turning the hips as my first move. It's as if my hips were in a barrel.

My left foot and left knee may actually move first, but the hips thought works for me. The lower body definitely leads the downswing as you unwind the coil you created on the backswing.

The start of the downswing must retain the left-side tension built up during the backswing. I feel tautness from the triceps of my left arm to the middle of my back. Ultimately that tension—and its release—create more arm and clubhead speed through the impact zone, which is how you hit the ball your maximum distance.

To hold this powerful coil starting the downswing, I feel my hips shift slightly toward the target and then unwind back to the left. They slide and turn simultaneously. As they do, my weight is moving onto my left foot. My left heel, pulled up on the backswing, returns to the ground in its original position.

My arms and shoulders, however, stay in virtually the same attitude they reached at the top of the swing. Their start down is delayed a bit; they stay turned and do not become active too soon.

You probably have heard the expression "coming over the top." It's a move that causes more damage than typhoons. The player who comes over the top starts turning his shoulders toward the target too early in the downswing. His arms come down outside the plane of the backswing and swing the clubhead into the ball on an outside-to-inside path. The most common result is a weak slice. The downswing really begins from below the waist. Then you won't come over the top. Your left forearm begins to rotate dramatically about halfway down. It is in the process of squaring the clubface at impact.

A lot of fairly good players try to start everything down together: feet, hips, arms, shoulders. I made the mistake of trying to do that myself for several years with no great success. If you start everything down together, there is a strong tendency to throw the clubhead at the ball with the right hand too soon, dissipating your power and not helping your accuracy, either. I converted to starting down with the lower body and became both longer and straighter.

Tempo is crucial in starting the downswing. It should be a gradual shifting of gears from backswing to forward swing. The transition must be smooth and relaxed. It's an easier but more powerful way to swing.

Weekend players often ask me if they should pause or stop the club at the top of the swing. I believe the golf swing should be a continuous, flowing motion. I don't like the idea of stopping noticeably at the top, but I'd rather see you pause slightly up there than make a quick, jerky change of directions. Too many people take the club back extra slowly, then rush the downswing as if they had

to catch a train about to pull out of the station. Ideally, you change directions from backswing to downswing at the same, controlled speed.

Curtis Strange makes the transition from backswing to downswing better than anyone else.

The very best players actually start forward with the lower body before the upper body has quite completed the backswing. The club is still moving back as the lower body moves toward the target, and the legs are well into the downswing by the time the upper body begins to work. But that sequence requires exquisite timing. I don't recommend it to most players.

I prefer to think about finishing the backswing, then starting down with the hips. It's possible to move the lower body too fast on the downswing, in which case the arms never catch up or you overuse your shoulders, but I don't see that happening much with weekend players. They usually need to think more about the lower body starting down.

**Best transition from
backswing to downswing:
Curtis Strange**

Swinging on down to the ball, I concentrate on swinging my arms past my head. My head should stay behind the ball through impact. A stable head improves your balance and means your club will come into the ball along the target line with your arms swinging freely.

You have to swing your arms fast! That's how you get clubhead speed and distance. If you make a solid move to your left side on the downswing, you can swing your arms as fast as you want. Your arms cannot move as fast as your feet. If your feet are working, you are free to unleash your arms and accelerate the clubhead into the hitting zone.

Golfers wonder when the hands and wrists should uncock. The hands and wrists cannot begin to release the club too early as long as your weight has shifted onto your left foot and your hips continue to turn. Don't worry about unhinging the hands and wrists—centrifugal force causes that to happen naturally. It's a result of retaining your left-side tension starting down.

Most golfers stay over on the right foot too long, throw the right shoulder outward and hit from the top. Their shots lack both power and direction.

Move firmly to your left foot and go ahead and *HIT* the ball. You can hit hard with your right hand. I hit the hell out of the ball with my right hand. But my left side is leading. At impact my left forearm has rotated back to its address position and squared the clubface. If my left hand was on that table, it would be upright. The wrist is firm, which lets you hit aggressively with the right hand.

If you're a dominantly right-sided person, you may have to feel that your right side is taking over on the downswing . . . that you're throwing the clubhead at the ball with your right hand. But make the goal of your downswing to get your left arm back into the position it occupied when you addressed the ball. This thought will help your rhythm and keep your right arm on track.

There are some very good right-sided players. Lanny Wadkins really fires his right side on the downswing. His left side is just guiding and hanging on. If you strive to keep your left arm close to your body swinging down, as Lanny does, you can hit the daylights out of the ball with your right side.

If your arms separate from your body, though, you're in trouble. Your arms will have to pull left and stay close to your body swinging down into the ball. If you feel a space in your left armpit, you're out of sync.

We talked about wanting the left knee pointing to the right of the ball at the top of the swing. At impact, I want the right knee pointing to the left of the ball.

At impact I feel my feet are almost flat on the ground, where they were at address. I know my weight is moving left and I'm beginning to roll onto the outside of my left foot, but I have the solid sensation that I've returned to my address position. My weight, mainly on my right heel at the top of the swing, is mainly on my left heel now.

**Best position through impact: Nick Price**

I've given you a lot of thoughts and feelings about the downswing, considering that it is a reflexive action. Try them on the practice tee and see if you feel what I'm talking about. Remember that you're after a happy blending of body parts and you want to swing in good balance.

Do you slice your longer shots?

If so, you aren't releasing the club through the hitting zone. Your clubhead speed and accuracy both suffer. Certainly you will never hit the ball as far off the tee as you are capable of hitting it.

In a good swing, release happens naturally, through centrifugal force. The clubhead gets heavier, in effect, as it's swung, and the wrists are unhinged at the right time to square the clubface to the ball. I release the club by rotating my forearms. I feel a pulling sensation in my left arm.

Most of you don't find release happening naturally and need to create it. You need to make it happen. Here's an easy-to-remember way to hit through the ball and release the club. It will encourage you to hook the ball, which will help slicers in particular.

*Try to touch your left forearm with your right forearm as you hit the ball.* When you're practicing, rotate your forearms as fast as you can in making this effort. Keep them relaxed so you can move them quickly.

Your forearms probably won't actually touch, but the attempt will lead to a better release. Work on it and you will stop steering the ball.

At this stage of the swing you have no conscious control of the clubhead. But concentrating on release before you start to swing can alleviate a tendency to steer or "block" your shots.

By the time my arms have swung through to horizontal, my left forearm should have rotated the club to an emphatic release. If my left hand was on the tabletop, the back of my hand would be flat. Most players rotate the club fairly naturally on the backswing, but fail to rotate it back through the ball, which is a major reason they slice.

Your preswing basics can promote an emphatic release. I prefer a strong grip to a weak grip for most players. If you don't have athletic arms, you will not be able to turn the club over at the bottom of the swing with a weak grip. The left hand will break down into a cupped position, which is the worst position you can be in through impact. A strong grip helps you release the club and hit the ball from right to left instead of slicing it. You should play with as strong a grip as you can get away with.

An adjustment in your stance at address also can lead to a better release. After you set up to the ball, pull your right foot back a bit. You will turn your hips better going back and release the club better coming through.

A good thought is to make the toe of the club pass the heel through the impact zone.

If you make the toe pass the heel through the ball you'll be delivering a strong, offensive blow instead of a timid, defensive one. The correct swing path sees the club come into the ball from inside the target line, travel along that line as it contacts the ball, then swing back inside the line after impact. If you fail to

rotate your forearms, the club won't swing back inside the line. The toe will not pass the heel.

Look on the swing as a mirror image—halfway back and halfway through. The right arm folds on the backswing as the left arm extends, then on the through-swing the left arm folds as the right arm extends.

Most weekend players fail to let the right arm fold enough going back or the left arm fold enough coming through. You can control and release the club easier if you keep your right elbow close to your side on the backswing and your left elbow close to your side on the through-swing.

The swing isn't precisely a mirror image because centrifugal force unloads on the downswing and throws the right arm forcefully toward the target. Both arms should be straight shortly after impact.

Another way to visualize this is to think of a clock. Your swing positions at 3 o'clock and 9 o'clock, halfway back and halfway through, should be very similar. Most of the left forearm rotation, back and through, has taken place. Your arms are close to your body and your head behind the ball. (Common post-impact mistakes are for the head to slide forward and/or for the left arm to come away from the chest.)

One final mental picture. Watch a power hitter in baseball. He releases his bat the way you need to release a golf club. His right forearm rolls over his left. Swinging a golf club like a baseball bat is a good drill.

Best release:
Payne Stewart

# THE FINISH

The big swing change on the PGA Tour in the last few years has come in the follow-through. More and more good tour players are finishing with the arms and club lower and more around the body. Curtis Strange and Fred Couples are two dramatic examples. It's something I've been working on. Even Jack Nicklaus, the high priest of the high finish, has flattened his follow-through.

A big advantage is that the arms and clubface stay on plane better. The swing is more circular—more of a Hula-Hoop in shape.

Most of us were taught to make a high arm finish. We were told to "reach for the sky" on the follow-through. Nicklaus and I formerly finished in that popular "reverse C" position. We looked like the letter C turned around. I have to think that's a major reason my game deteriorated and Jack has had so much painful back trouble. Sam Snead never finished in that "reverse C" position—and he never has had back trouble.

The high finish can be caused by putting too much emphasis on extending the club down the target line through the ball. That creates tension and keeps the club from swinging naturally back inside the line after impact. You don't release the club well. You curtail your clubhead speed. The tendency is to block or slice the ball out to the right.

It's too easy to think of the swing as being excessively upright, or vertical. The club can be swung more repetitively and faster on a circular route than on a straight line. Think of a tilted circle. You make a deeper backswing turn, and you turn more with your body coming through the ball. Your arms and the club follow your body pivot.

If a perfectly upright swing were a Ferris wheel at an amusement park and a perfectly flat swing were a merry-go-round, your swing should be in between those two extremes. Your lower body doesn't have to be as active in a flatter swing. It turns but it doesn't slide much. If you do a lot of sliding with your lower body, you'll have to time your hit very precisely with your arms and hands.

In an upright power swing, you get to the top and then drive your legs and try to catch up with your arms before you get to the ball. That was Nicklaus for years. You can catch up with the arms if you're strong and supple. If you're not, I recommend a flatter swing and flatter follow-through.

A relatively strong grip helps. A player like Couples likes to try to get the club around onto his shoulder at the finish. That's a far cry from the old "hands high" finish, and it's a much more relaxed and natural position.

Your finish position is simply the culmination of all that has gone before it in your swing. You don't hit the ball with your follow-through, but studying your follow-through can be tremendously instructive. Ideally, your weight will have shifted entirely onto your left foot. *You should be able to lift your right foot and stay in balance.*

I don't want to feel any weight on my right toe at the finish. My weight has

**Best finish:
Fred Couples**

rolled onto the outside of my left foot, more toward the heel than the toe.

Another checkpoint I apply to my finish position is that my bellybutton faces my target, or slightly left of my target. That tells me my hips have turned properly swinging down. (Early in my career I checked my belt buckle, but now I wear beltless slacks.)

What are the common bad finishes and what do they indicate? If you finish with your left foot flat on the ground and pointing at the target, you have made a hated reverse weight shift and fallen back on the downswing. You left too much weight on your left side going back, then your weight had to shift to your right side coming down. That's just the opposite of the weight shift you want.

You have to make a better turn behind the ball on the backswing to avoid this problem. Put more weight on your right side when you address the ball. Set up with your right eye over your right knee. Now you're preconditioned to get your weight behind the ball. Turn around your right leg going back.

Another cause of the reverse weight shift is scooping at the ball in a futile attempt to get it airborne. Trust the loft of the club to do that job. Work on making a more descending blow. On your iron shots off the turf, try to take a divot in front of the ball.

If you fall forward toward the target line in your follow-through, you probably used your upper body too soon on the forward swing. You are trying to force distance by using the slow big muscles of your upper body instead of the quicker muscles of your arms and legs.

Here's a gambit for swinging in better balance. Try to hold your finish position until the ball lands. It's a good mental device to use on the course. Rather than worry about the mechanics of your swing, simply try to be in balance on every shot. When you hit a shot, hold your follow-through posture as if you were posing for a picture. If you find yourself unable to hold your follow-through, you are overswinging and failing to shift your weight well.

You will have to adjust and swing at a slower, smoother pace, because you cannot swing faster than you can stay in balance. This is especially the case with uneven lies. Make a practice swing from an uphill, downhill or sidehill lie and see if you can hold your finish. If you cannot, throttle back.

It can help your swing over all to visualize a good follow-through as you set up for a shot. My primary thought is to finish with all my weight on my left foot so I could lift my right foot and stay in balance.

**Best tempo:
Sam Snead**

We've been going through the mechanics of the full swing step-by-step, from grip to follow-through. They all are vitally important to making solid, consistent contact with the ball and scoring well. But it's also terribly important to be able to meld these individual mechanics into a cohesive, flowing whole.

Good swing tempo (or overall pace) lets your mechanics work for you during your swing in the proper sequence. It can even compensate for poor mechanics to some extent, since with good tempo you can give yourself time to make compensations as you swing.

Smoothness comes from an absence of tension at the start. I talk about tension in the swing, but that means a good tension or tautness that you build by stretching and winding the muscles. I don't mean the tension at address which stifles your muscles and causes a jerky swing. With this kind of tension you usually end up swinging too fast at the wrong time. When that happens, your balance is the first thing to go and a poor shot almost always results.

Poor posture usually creates tension at address. But you can be too tight even with a setup that is positionally correct. I like to overcome this tightness by building in a feeling of pace, of being in control of my swing, before I ever step up to the ball. I think about good tempo.

I happen to have a fast swing, but it's not so fast that the movements can't happen in correct sequence. It's possible to swing the club too slowly, but I hardly ever see that happen, especially with weekend players. Almost every golfer would play better if he slowed down his swing.

I think the most important thing in slowing down your swing is to work with one simple, graphic image. It should be a positive thought about good rhythm.

I prefer a "feel" thought to a "mechanical" thought—especially on the course—and I prefer an "overall swing" thought to a "partial swing" thought.

You really shouldn't concern yourself that much with the position of the club when you're trying to slow down your swing. It's better to have one good image

of a rhythmic swing in mind before you ever address the ball.

Just a quick physical aside: You have to be relaxed to swing smoothly. Be sure your forearms feel loose. If your forearms are stiff, the club will never be set at the top the same way twice.

When you have trouble with your rhythm and need to relax, maybe you should do everything in your preshot routine a little more slowly. Set your feet in position more slowly, waggle the club more slowly. Again, though, I recommend that you concentrate on finding one image of good rhythm that clicks for you, because to me that's the key to slowing down the swing. There are all kinds of thoughts you can consider. I'm going to give you a few that work for me and could, I believe, apply to anyone. I hope you'll experiment with them in practice and find one that helps you.

My favorite key for slowing down the swing is just to think of Sam Snead swinging a club. All I have to do is picture his nice, flowing action, and my swing gets smoother. In my view, he still has the best rhythm of anybody who has ever played the game. Gene Littler comes pretty close, but I think Sam's rhythm is the sweetest.

I always look forward to playing in the Masters in April, because I can still go watch Sam practice. He's an honorary starter and still a marvel to watch and study. He was my father's swing model, and he's always been mine, too.

Sam's swing may not be mechanically perfect—his clubface doesn't stay square all the way through the swing and his leg action was never the greatest—but his classic tempo more than makes up for any imperfections. He has always swung well within himself, never forcing a shot. He wants his swing to feel "oily." Sam's always said that a long swing is the one that lasts. He always worked hard at keeping his backswing long, so his tempo would be smooth.

In this age of high-tech video equipment, every golfer's game room should include a film or tape of Sam's swing. His tempo is contagious.

I heard a memorable tempo tip not long ago from an average golfer. He said he's never had a lesson, but he plays respectably thinking only about a word from "The Sound of Music"—edelweiss, the name of a flower that grows in the Alps. He swings back and forth to the three syllables of the word. The first syllable takes him about halfway to the top of his swing, the second syllable to

the top, and the third syllable down to impact. Ed-el-weiss. Back and forth. Ed-el-weiss. I've been trying it myself. I've always loved that musical.

Another good, simple image is to picture a pendulum (or a metronome) swinging. A golf club can and should act like a pendulum. Think of a pendulum going back up, stopping briefly and starting down smoothly. It literally comes to a dead halt, and I want my golf swing to do the same thing at the top, or else it's moving too fast. I want the club to feel like a pendulum as I swing it.

Amateurs usually make the mistake of speeding up their swings with the longer clubs. You should try to swing every club at the same easy pace. It will take a little longer to swing the long clubs, but your tempo should not speed up.

Nick Faldo did a videotape in which he hit 15 different shots with five different clubs. You could see that he swung with the same tempo every time. He says swing tempo has been the most important factor in his career. He believes it relieves the pressure and stress of the game.

If you watch Faldo in action, you'll notice that he always makes his practice swings with good tempo. Then when he addresses a real shot, he tries to duplicate that tempo.

The start of your swing pretty much determines your tempo. If you're fast away from the ball, you probably will lose control.

It's one of golf's great clichés that you should start your backswing slowly. It ought to be just as great a cliché that you should start your downswing slowly.

Our goal is to build clubhead speed through the ball. If you start the downswing as if it were a 100-yard dash, you expend your power too soon. The pace you want in your swing is more like a mile runner's—save your energy for a strong finishing kick. Al Geiberger, who has exquisite tempo, says you are allowed only one fast moment in your swing. It better come late in your downswing. The only time you should rush your swing is from about waist high coming into the ball.

If you're a typical weekend golfer, you may well have no clear idea how fast you are swinging. Here's a test. *You should be able to feel the weight and momentum of the clubhead during the swing.* Otherwise you're over the speed limit.

**Let's look at Sam Snead's swing in close-up photography.**

# FOOTWORK

My feeling—and it's literally a physical sensation—is that the timing of the swing starts from the feet. I feel with my feet. They are my connection to the ground, and they tell me if I'm swinging in sync. You can make a well-coordinated swing only if your lower body is alive and active. If you don't use your feet, the club won't go back on an arc; you pick it up with your hands.

*Your weight should go mainly to your right heel at the top of the swing, then mainly to your left heel at impact.*

Good footwork will prevent the hated reverse weight shift, in which your center of gravity shifts left on your backswing and the weight never gets over to the right heel.

Letting the left heel come up on the backswing is a good way to make a fuller turn. Just be sure you don't overdo it, and be sure you replant it where it was.

I keep my weight on the insides of my feet. Those are my pressure points. From address to impact, the weight should not drift to the outsides of your feet. I start with my weight pretty evenly distributed between my feet. Then it goes solidly to my right heel at the top, solidly to my left heel at impact. I'm anything but flat-footed, but I stay on the insides of my feet.

My checkpoint at the top is that there should be no daylight under the ball of my right foot—no spikes showing. If you can see air or spikes under the inside of your shoe, you've gone too far.

At impact, my checkpoint is to *move my left knee over my left foot.* My knee has moved inside on the backswing, pointing behind the ball at the top, and now swings directly over the foot. That's where I want to time my hit.

I've always used Sam Snead's footwork as a model. He's never been out of rhythm in his life. Al Geiberger has great footwork, too. Among my contemporaries, Seve Ballesteros has wonderful footwork. Watch his feet the next chance you get.

If the timing of my swing is off, I concentrate on my footwork to get it back.

Your weight goes to your
right heel at the top of the
swing, to your left heel at
impact. My swing thought
through the ball is to get my
left knee over my left foot.

Maybe the biggest fault I see in the average golfer's swing is inflexible knees. I'll be frank. Most of you have cement legs. Your footwork is poor and your lower bodies don't work. Consequently your upper bodies tend to bob up and down and your hands get too active.

I like to give people with this problem a quick fix that I call the left-knee, right-knee move. It can reverse a lot of bad tendencies.

Just point your left knee to the right of the ball at the top of your swing, and point your right knee to the left of the ball at impact. Left knee, right knee.

This move will encourage you to turn your hips and shift your weight back and forth with no conscious effort. It's possible to use your hips, knees and feet too much—but hardly any weekend player does.

Try to keep your knees consistently flexed from the time you address the ball until you've hit it. If you set up with locked knees, you have no chance to make a good swing. You're stuck before you start. A likely effect is pointing your left knee straight out toward the

**Point your left knee to the right of the ball at the top of your swing.**

ball on your backswing. There is no greater swing-wrecker.

Get a little aggressive with your knees! Start from a good foundation and move those knees! Move them in harmony with the rest of your swing, but move them!

Move your knees on short swings as well as full swings. We all are prone to hit little chips and pitches with only our arms, and it doesn't work. You need some motion down below.

The best drill I've seen for improving your knee action is the Mehlhorn Drill, named for a colorful old tour player, Wild Bill Mehlhorn. It's in the chapter on drills.

When you make a full swing, point the left knee to the right of the ball on your backswing, and point your right knee to the left of the ball at impact. Left knee, right knee.

**Point your right knee to the left of the ball at impact.**

Don't be afraid to whip the club through the ball forcefully and *HIT* the ball.

Most golfers are too conservative swinging the club. They swing to the ball and quit on the shot. You have to swing past the ball.

We've been isolating the basics of the swing in this book. Work on these fundamentals on the practice range. But when you're on the course playing a round of golf, don't confuse yourself thinking about eight different mechanics and swing positions. Think about swinging freely. Release that clubhead. Be a little reckless.

Turn that body away from the ball a lot. And turn it through a lot. Flex your knees and let them work. Speed up your arms on the downswing. Swing the club as fast as you find you can without losing control of it.

Obviously you don't want to swing out of control, but too many of us are tentative about hitting the ball. Learn how quickly your body can move. Find the rhythm that will keep your arms, shoulders and hips in sync while producing extra power. Think about releasing the club. Once you develop the timing of a proper release, you'll play much more assertively.

Golfers often tell each other to "swing easy." It can be useful advice. But you'll never play good golf if you don't learn to hit the ball hard. You won't drive it far enough or spin your irons enough. A pro like Payne Stewart may not look as if he's swinging hard, but his swing is so smooth it fools you into thinking he's lazy. Believe me, Payne swings hard. So does Ian Woosnam, another smooth swinger.

A good indoor training idea is to swing a weighted bar as if it were a golf club. Use a short, heavy bar so you don't ruin any furniture. Swing it down and through as fast as you can. It will help your release.

Trapshooting is one of my favorite hobbies. I started nailing a lot more birds when my coach told me to "Get reckless!" You have to swing the gun past the clay target aggressively, leading it. The golf swing requires the same kind of uninhibited action.

Give a golfer one wish—in any language—and he almost surely will ask to hit the ball 20 yards farther. It's the universal dream. Is there a greater joy than driving it past your biggest rival on a long hole? That's the shot you'll talk about in the locker room later. That's the big ego booster.

Every golfer I know wants to hit the ball farther, including me. My main distance key is turning the right hip. I think about taking my right-front pants pocket and putting it behind me.

If you *turn your right hip out of the way* early in the swing, a lot of good things will happen. Your shoulders turn more easily and work in tandem with your hips. The club swings back inside the target line and around the body, rather than outside and up, which causes a slice. The big muscles coil powerfully, and you'll feel the freedom to go ahead and rip the ball.

The player who turns the right hip most dramatically is Jack Nicklaus. Watch Lanny Wadkins and Greg Norman, too. Greg is the longest straight driver today, I think.

Another key thought I invoke to drive the ball farther is to make a slower, larger shoulder turn. That gives me time and room to build power.

You cannot be tense and hit a big drive. If you're tight, your swing will be short and jerky. I keep my forearms relaxed, so I can make a bigger turn and whip the clubhead through the ball, making a dramatic release.

To add distance you must either generate more clubhead speed at impact or create more solid impact, or both.

Since most golfers tend to strike glancing blows, improving your contact might be the best way for you to add length. If you can catch the ball on the center of the clubface with the club moving down your intended line, you'll get maximum distance from the force you've generated.

Moreover, better contact means that more of your shots with a given club will go a consistent distance. Merely adding clubhead speed, so that you can swing a 6-iron instead of a 5-iron from 150 yards out, is counterproductive if your 6-iron shots sometimes go 160 yards and sometimes go only 130 yards.

A longer driver also can be helpful. You might want to try a 45-inch driver, an inch and a half longer than normal. The bigger swing arc you get with the longer club can mean more clubhead speed. Be sure to stand a little farther away from the ball with a longer driver. And you absolutely must not rush your downswing. Be patient with a long club. Wait on it.

I'm not sure how conclusive the equipment tests are when it comes to using a metal driver and a two-piece ball, but I know a lot of our senior pros in America swear by the combination. To some extent it's true today that you can *buy* added yardage.

**Best power move:
Ian Woosnam**

# SWING
# IMAGERY

A good golf swing is greater than the sum of its parts. Euclid didn't say that, but he should have. Much modern golf instruction is mechanical and fragmented. We are urged to think about the knees, or the right elbow, or even the left big toe. All those aspects are important, but only if they blend into a whole that transcends their individuality.

It's all right to concentrate on separate mechanics on the practice tee. But on the course you'd better forget everything except cohesiveness. After all, it takes only about two seconds to make a golf swing, and that's not enough time to put one together like a jigsaw puzzle.

Learn to make this distinction when thinking about your swing: Part-swing thoughts are for the practice range. Full-swing thoughts are for the golf course.

Bobby Jones once said that when he was playing well he thought of only one thing. And when he was playing *really* well he thought of nothing at all. There's a lot of wisdom there.

Following are several full-swing thoughts I have used over the years to good advantage. See if they help you pull your swing mechanics together.

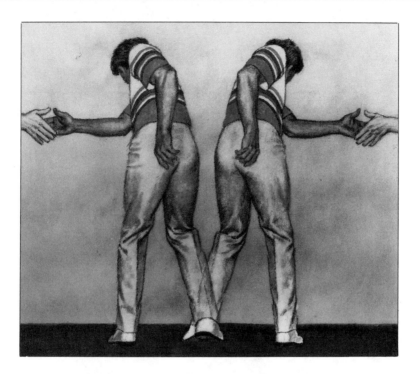

## 'SHAKE HANDS' FOR A SIMPLE SWING

We all make the golf swing too complicated. My dad has always told me the swing is as simple as shaking hands. You shake hands with your left hand on the backswing, then with your right hand swinging through.

Take your address position, with your upper body bent over and your knees flexed. Now turn 90 degrees to your right and pretend you are shaking some-one's hand left-handed, waist high. Your left arm extends, your left knee works inward, your hips turn out of the way. Do the same thing in reverse going through. Your right arm extends, your right knee shifts toward the ball, your hips clear. That's the golf swing, in essence.

I correlate this shaking-hands image with the concept of rotating the left forearm, halfway back and halfway through. The shaking-hands image is a right-handed emphasis for releasing the club through the ball. Or you can combine the two thoughts and hit the ball with your left forearm and right hand. Just be sure you rotate the left forearm so the action of the right hand doesn't break down the left wrist.

A good drill is to make slow-motion half swings in front of a mirror, rotating the left forearm and shaking hands. The toe of the clubhead should point up halfway back and point up again halfway through.

## THINK OF THE SWING AS A CIRCLE

When I have played my best, all I thought about was keeping the club on the right path. Visualizing that path becomes simpler if you think of the swing as a tilted circle around your body. It is not a perfect circle—the clubhead starts away from the ball on a straight line, then swings inside that line and up, and it returns to the ball on a path slightly lower and more inside the backswing path. But it is close to a circle.

Since the swing is a circular movement, the path of the clubhead on the forward swing is from inside the target line before impact, and then back inside the line after impact. That inward movement of the clubhead after impact should happen naturally as your left arm swings left and begins to fold.

You will be able to release the club swinging it on this path—letting the toe of the club pass the heel through impact—and hit the ball farther and straighter.

Think of the swing as a circle.

## KEEP YOUR SPINE ANGLE STEADY

A helpful swing key is to establish a sound spine angle at address and maintain it through impact. If you can do that, a lot of good things will happen. Your head will stay quiet and your swing path will be good, to name two.

You establish your spine angle by standing up straight, then bending from the hips and flexing your knees. Your back is not at all slumped. Retain that upper-body angle during your swing.

Curtis Strange is a player whose spine angle stays very stable. His head moves laterally but does not bob up and down. It's a big reason he's so consistent.

I think about maintaining a "quiet" head throughout the swing. The old advice to keep the head down can be inhibiting if it causes rigidity and blocks your turn. It's okay for the head to move off the ball a bit so long as your spine angle remains stable.

## SWING AROUND THE BACK OF YOUR NECK

To keep my swing center steady, which maintains my balance, I feel as if I'm swinging around the back of my neck.

This especially stabilizes your backswing. It helps keep your weight from going to the outside of your right foot and prevents swaying to the right. It also helps avoid the other common fault on the backswing, which is hanging too much on the left side and failing to get enough of your weight to the right. This can cause you to lean left with your upper body as you swing back, resulting in a reverse weight shift and a weak blow.

On the forward swing, the thought of swinging around the back of your neck keeps you in balance by helping you stay behind the ball with your upper body. It keeps you from lurching to the left with your upper body and getting too much weight to your left too quickly. Your weight should be moving left during the forward swing, but it actually is about equally distributed at impact.

Swinging around the back of your neck can give you a solid feeling from takeaway to finish.

## FEEL THE CLUBHEAD

The most important thing I do if my game goes off is try to feel the weight of the clubhead during my swing.

If you swing too hard, you don't feel the clubhead. You'll do better if you play within yourself. Never swing the club 100 percent.

Try to feel the clubhead throughout your swing. That will help you stay in control.

You will feel the clubhead if you use the lightest grip pressure you can without the club slipping in your hands.

# DRILLS
# TO PRACTICE

Drills are a great way to ingrain your swing basics. They let you *feel* what we've been talking about in this book.

Drills can be fun as well as instructive. They make your practice varied and interesting.

The secret to improving your swing is to do drills regularly. Try to do them daily, for a few minutes at least. Ultimately you want to build into your swing the feelings your drills give you. Then you'll need the drills only as a refresher course, going back to them if your swing falters.

I've selected several swing drills that I especially like because they work for me and because they correct the most common swing faults I see in weekend golfers. There are dozens more drills, many of them quite specific to particular swing problems, that have been developed over the years by leading teachers and players.

Some of the drills that follow can be done indoors when the weather is poor.

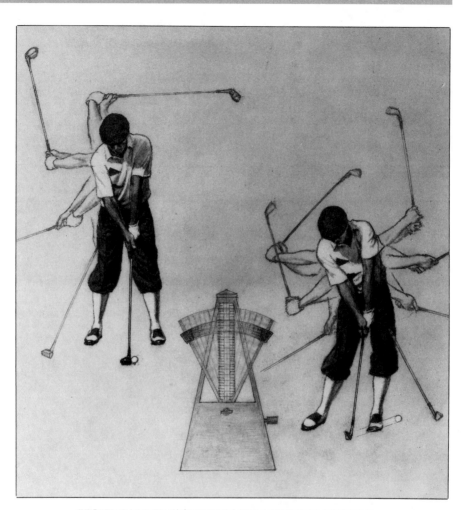

## HOW PAYNE STEWART PRACTICES TEMPO

When it comes to swing tempo, Payne Stewart can give a metronome a stroke a side. His tempo is probably the smoothest and most consistent on tour. Payne tries to swing every club at the same, unforced pace, from wedge through driver. He practices tempo by alternately hitting balls with short clubs and long clubs. He keeps his change of directions at the top of the swing as controlled with the long clubs as with the short ones.

Most golfers speed up their swings with the long clubs, and the results are often ruinous. When Payne faces a critical shot with a long club, he imagines he's swinging a short club. He wants the tempo the same, especially at the top of his swing.

## HAVE A SEAT—ALMOST

Here's an exercise that will strengthen your legs, so you can maintain your balance and your spine angle. You sit down—but without a chair. It's a good winter training drill.

Stand with your back flat against a wall, placing your feet about a foot from the wall and shoulder-width apart. Now slowly lower yourself into a sitting position by bending your knees, or come as close to a sitting position as you comfortably can.

Hold that position until it starts to hurt. You'll feel a burning sensation in your quadriceps. Then stop.

Do the sitting exercise a few times a day and you will build a stronger foundation for your swing.

## LIFT LEFT LEG TO SHIFT WEIGHT BETTER

Here's a drill to improve your balance, your weight shift and your power. Make practice swings lifting your left foot off the ground on your backswing and replanting it as you start your downswing.

You see home-run hitters in baseball lift the left foot. They can coil more fully and then uncoil more forcefully.

It probably will take you a few tries to do this drill well. Work up to really turning your back to the target and timing your release of the clubhead through impact. You'll get behind the ball better and swing through it better.

If you don't mind looking a little different, this drill is a good way to make a practice swing on the course.

### THE FEET-TOGETHER DRILL

This one probably promotes more good swing results than almost any other drill. Some of the best players in the world have practiced swinging with their feet together, from Bobby Jones to Jack Nicklaus.

The feet-together drill encourages you to swing your arms and turn your body, rather than sway from side to side. Your shoulders respond to the swinging of your arms.

Start with a short iron on the range with the ball teed. Swing slowly at first, gradually increasing your pace as you gain a better sense of balance. (You'll be surprised how far you can hit the ball with a little work!)

Gradually widen your stance and work up to longer clubs—but remember how you felt with your feet together. If you lose that feeling, revert to practicing with your feet together until you regain your balance and timing.

## THE MEHLHORN DRILL FOR FREER LEG ACTION

I've said earlier that perhaps the biggest fault I see in average golfers' swings is inflexible knees, or cement legs. Your lower bodies don't function enough.

The best drill I've seen for improving your lower-body action is to hold a club at both ends across your thighs and move your feet and legs as you would during a swing. The shaft must stay against your legs. If it comes away from your legs, you are not moving well.

## LEADBETTER'S PIVOT DRILL

Teacher David Leadbetter strongly believes that the pivot action of the body is the base for a good swing. He compares it to the rotary action of a discus thrower coiling and uncoiling.

His favorite drill, especially for new golfers, is a pivot drill. He asks you to put your right hand on your left shoulder and your left hand on your right shoulder, and turn back and forth. That's the essence of the swing in his method.

David urges us to check our turns in a mirror. With your back to the mirror, swing an imaginary club to the top of your swing, turning so you can look at yourself in the mirror. Your trunk should be coiled. Your hips should be level. Your weight should be primarily on your right heel, so no daylight shows under the inside of the right shoe. Your left knee should point at the ball or a bit behind it. That's a good pivot, and you're ready to unleash a powerful, controlled downswing.

## GRIP THE CLUB AT THE WRONG END

No doubt you know the abject frustration of losing your swing. We all do. You've been playing well, but suddenly the wheels come off.

A good way to regain your feel is to grip the club at the clubhead end and make a few practice swings. This makes the club feel very, very light. It gives you a different sensation with your hands, and improves your grip pressure.

When you go back to gripping the club normally, you'll automatically be able to feel the clubhead, which is the most important thing you can try to do during the swing.

Swing the club gripping the clubhead end—and get the wheels back on. I've done it during a round on tour more than once.

# FACE-ON

The edge of the left hand would be
on the tabletop.

The left forearm has rotated to its
maximum, and the left hand is
"shaking hands."

The left wrist is firm at impact.
The left hand would be on its edge
on the table.

The left forearm has made its 180-degree rotation. The right hand is "shaking hands."

# DOWN THE LINE

The left forearm is not quite fully
rotated, but the left hand is in
"shaking-hands" position.

The left forearm rotates no farther
than this.

Now the left forearm is pouring it
on. I can hit hard with my right
hand.

The left-forearm rotation is done, and I'm "shaking hands" with my right hand.

# FROM
# THE
# REAR

The left hand says "Hello, glad to meet you!"

The right hand says "Hello, glad to
meet you!" The back of the left
hand is flat on the table.

# FROM
# THE
# TARGET

The left forearm has rotated, and
the left hand is "shaking hands."

The left-forearm rotation begins at
about this point in the downswing.

The back of the left hand would be
flat on the table.

# OVERHEAD

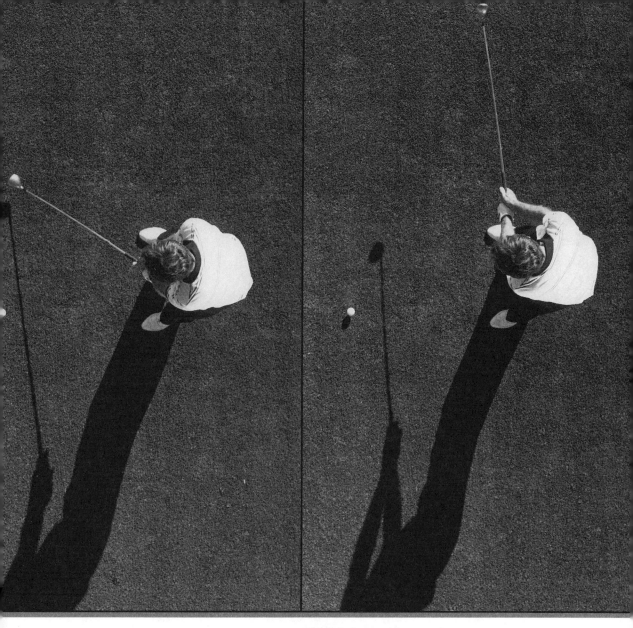

The left forearm has nearly
completed its backswing rotation.
The left hand is almost in the
"shaking-hands" position.

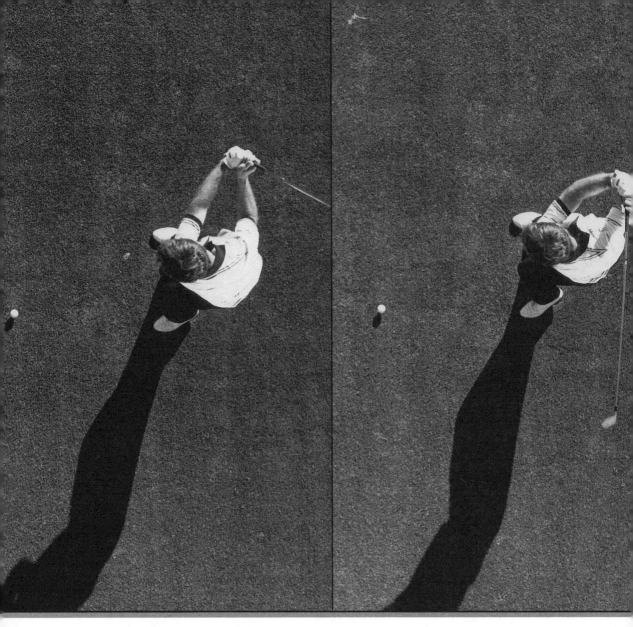

With the rotation of the left
forearm complete, the left arm lifts
the club to the top.

The right hand is in the "shaking-
hands" position. The rotation of
the left forearm is finished.